FIRES AND FLOODS

K[illegible]ERS

SCHOLASTIC IN[illegible]
New York Toronto London Auc[illegible]nd Sydney
Mexico City New Delhi Hong Kong Buenos Aires

Photo Credits:
Front Cover: © tim gartside/Alamy; Back Cover: © Andrew Holbrooke/Corbis.
Page 1: © PhotoSpin, Inc/Alamy; page 3: © Jim Erickson/CORBIS; page 4: © Macduff Everton/Corbis; page 5: © Jim West/Alamy; page 6–7: © Arco Images/Alamy; page 7 inset: © David R. Frazier Photolibrary, Inc./Alamy; page 8: Dr. Vic Bradbury/Photo Researchers, Inc.; page 9: © Andre Jenny/Alamy; page 10: © JUPITERIMAGES/Brand X/Alamy; page 11: © Michael Beiriger/Alamy; page 12: © A.T. Willett/Alamy; page 13: © James L. Amos/Corbis; pages 14–15: © Digital Vision/Alamy; page 16: © A.T. Willett/Alamy; page 17: © WorldFoto/ Alamy; pages 18–19: © Jan Baks/Alamy; page 20: © Blend Images/Alamy; page 21: © Dinodia Images/Alamy; page 22: © Andrew Holbrooke/Corbis; page 23: © Andre Jenny/Alamy; page 24 inset: © M. Timothy O'Keefe/Alamy; pages 24–25: © PhotoSpin, Inc/Alamy; page 26: © John Prior Images/ Alamy; page 27: © Eye Ubiquitous/Alamy; pages 28–29: © LHB Photo/Alamy; page 29 inset: © Mikael Utterstrom/Alamy; page 30: © Keith Shuttlewood/Alamy; page 31: © Tony Kwan/Alamy.

ISBN-13: 978-0-545-07230-4
ISBN-10: 0-545-07230-1

Book design: Kay Petronio

Expert readers:
Fires: Gregory J. Waters, National Park Service
Floods: Dr. Keith L. Seitter, American Meteorological Society

12 11 10 9 8 7 6 5 4 3 2 8 9 10 11 12 13/0

Printed in the U.S.A.
First printing, October 2008

Fire and water are important. They can help us. But they can hurt us, too.

Fire gives us light so we can see. It warms us up. It gives us heat to cook our food.

All fires need fuel in order to burn. There are many types of fuel, such as wood, gas, oil, and coal. Wood is fuel for a campfire. Gas is fuel for cooking. It also keeps some homes warm. Oil and coal are fuel for big factory furnaces.

Trees, brush, and grass are fuel for forest fires. The trees and plants get very dry when there is no rain for a long time. It is easy for a fire to start.

SMOKEY
SMOKEY
FIRE DANGER
EXTREME
TODAY!
PREVENT FOREST FIRES

Forest fires can start in many ways. Lightning can cause a spark that lights a tree on fire. The air can get so hot that a fire starts when sap explodes inside a tree.

People can start forest fires, too. Campers can forget to put out their fires completely. They can be careless with matches. People who live near forests have to be careful with fires in barbecue grills.

A small fire can grow quickly if the wind is strong. Wind moves the flames from tree to tree.

Some fire is a natural part of the life of a forest. Fire cleans out dead brush by burning it to ash. Then animals that live in the forest can find food more easily. New plants and trees have more room and sunlight to grow.

A forest fire is dangerous when it burns close to where people live. Fire burns down houses and stores. It can destroy crops and pastures.

Experts watch the weather. They warn people when the danger of fire is high. U.S. Forest Service rangers watch the forests from mountaintops. They call firefighters when they see smoke.

Fighting forest fires is a hard job. Smoke is the biggest danger. It clouds the air so firefighters can't see. Smoke gets in their lungs. That makes it hard for them to breathe.

Firefighters sometimes fight fires from the air. They drop fire-stopping liquid called slurry from airplanes.

Firefighters on the ground spray water on the fire. They clear away brush and trees in front of the fire. They hope that the fire will stop when it runs out of fuel.

The trees and ground look dark and bare after a fire. But the ash from burned plants is like fertilizer. Plants and flowers begin to grow very quickly.

Seeds in the soil sprout. They grow into tall trees. The land will be a forest again.

Water is important for people, animals, and plants to stay alive. We drink water to stay healthy. We use water to wash ourselves and our clothes. We play in water and ride boats on lakes, rivers, or the ocean.

Water can be very powerful. It can flood towns and roads. A few inches of fast-moving water can carry away trees and cars. Rivers, streams, and lakes can flood. Ocean waves can flood towns along the coast.

Usually rainwater seeps into the ground. Sometimes there is a lot of rain, and pools of water start to form. The water spreads across the land. Flash floods happen when rain comes down faster than it can seep into the ground.

Floods also happen when the ground is frozen and water cannot seep into it. This usually happens in the mountains. Water moves downhill as snow melts and rain falls. Mountain streams flood houses and farms in the valleys below.

Hurricanes can cause floods. Hurricane winds push huge waves onto the shore. They bring heavy rain that falls for miles inland. Hurricane wind and water cause a lot of damage.

Tsunamis can cause floods. Tsunamis are waves caused by earthquakes or volcano eruptions on the ocean floor. The waves swamp the coast with very little warning.

People try to stop water from flooding in many ways. They dig out river bottoms so that the river can hold more water. They build huge basins, called reservoirs. These basins hold water for drinking or watering fields.

People also build levees to stop water from flooding. Levees are walls made of earth or concrete. They are built next to oceans and big rivers. People use sandbags to protect their houses when big levees break.

Many people live in areas where floods often happen. Some of them build their houses on stilts. Floodwaters can then flow right under the house.

Other people use pumps in their basements to remove the water. Hoses carry the water outside.

Some flooding is good for the earth. Floodwater carries dirt that is rich with minerals. The dirt is left behind when the water withdraws. The minerals make the dirt, or soil, good for growing crops.

It may take a while to recover from a flood. But the land will dry over time. Then people will repair roads, bridges, levees, and houses.

Glossary

brush—small trees, low plants, and bushes

crop—a plant grown in large amounts, usually for food

fertilizer—a substance that makes soil richer and helps plants and trees grow better

fuel—a source of heat or energy

furnace—a large enclosed metal chamber in which fuel is burned to produce heat

inland—areas of land away from an ocean coast

mineral—a substance found in nature that is not a plant or an animal

pasture—grazing land for animals

seep—to flow or trickle slowly

spark—a quick flash of light and heat

stilts—poles that hold buildings above the ground or water level